Grades 1-3

SCHOLASTIC

Reading Response
Bookmarks &
Graphic Organizers

Reproducible Learning Tools That Prompt Students to Reflect on Text
During and After Reading to Maximize Comprehension

by Kim Blaise

New York ○ Toronto ○ London ○ Auckland ○ Sydney
New Delhi ○ Mexico City ○ Hong Kong ○ Buenos Aires

Teaching
Resources

To Karen McNally, for getting me started,

Jill Rogovic and Lisa McKeon, for making it better,

and my students, for keeping me on my toes!

Editor: Karen Kellaher
Cover design: Jason Robinson
Interior design: Grafica, Inc.
Interior illustrations: Teresa Anderko, Steve Cox, and Maxie Chambliss
ISBN: 978-0-545-21185-7
Copyright © 2012 by Kim Blaise
All rights reserved. Published by Scholastic Inc.
Printed in the U.S.A.

1 2 3 4 5 6 7 8 9 10   40   19 18 17 16 15 14 13 12

Table of Contents

Introduction

The Life-Changing Bookmark

Have you ever been to a workshop that transformed your teaching immediately? That moment occurred for me when I attended a workshop in Westchester, New York, run by LitLife, a consulting group that brings innovative approaches to literacy education into schools across the country. The presenter, Karen McNally, introduced our group to something she called a "retelling string," a piece of yarn with all sorts of buttons glued onto it. There was a button shaped like a book, another in the shape of a person, and several other buttons, too. Karen read a picture book aloud to the group, then invited us to use the special string to help her retell the story. We all held the book-shaped button as we recalled the title and author. We moved on to the person button as we discussed the main characters. Step by step, story element by story element, we recalled and retold the important parts of the tale. By the end of the workshop, my heart was racing, and I couldn't wait to get back in my classroom. I knew this was one literacy tool that I needed to re-create and use with my students immediately. (More information on Karen McNally's wonderful retelling string can be found in the book she wrote with Pam Allyn entitled *The Complete Year in Reading and Writing: Kindergarten* [Scholastic, 2008].)

After making my own retelling strings using braided yarn, a hot glue gun, and buttons and wood shapes from a local craft store, I enthusiastically put them to work in my grade 2 classroom. Within months, "touching and retelling" became a cornerstone of our language arts curriculum.

Once I saw how effectively the strings helped students focus on important story elements, I was tempted to send the retelling strings home for use during homework and just-for-fun reading. I decided that I'd make portable "strings" on paper rather than send the original classroom strings home. I created them on the computer, printed them on card stock, and covered them in contact paper for durability. They made perfect bookmarks for my busy, developing readers.

A Big Hit

Within months of implementing the retelling strings and bookmarks, my loftiest hopes were realized. My students became better able to talk about their reading. It was clear that they were thinking about the characters, settings, and plots of the books they read. They were making and refining predictions. They were even making incredible connections to other pieces of literature and to their own lives. I was astonished when my quietest student, a girl I'll call Adriana, used the retelling strings and bookmarks to find her voice. Before, Adriana had rarely raised her hand. When she did speak, more vocal classmates frequently interrupted her. But with her retelling string or bookmark in her hand, Adriana was able to speak up and retell what she had read. Adriana's finger

on her bookmark was an indicator to my other students that Adriana had the floor. It was like putting a microphone in her hand!

I wasn't the only one to notice the change. Notes and phone calls began pouring in from parents, grandparents, and tutors thanking me for the bookmarks and asking for extra copies. During one summer session, I introduced the retelling bookmarks to some students who hadn't been in my class the previous year. I soon got a grateful phone call from the mother of one student. According to this mom, her son had never been able to retell or summarize a story; he could not decide what was important to include. The bookmark helped him focus right in on the fundamental story elements.

Since the fiction bookmark did such wonders in helping my students talk about stories, it seemed only natural to expand the idea. In collaboration with my second-grade colleague, Jill Rogovic, I decided to create a similar bookmark for nonfiction. Instead of characters, plot, and setting, this bookmark invited students to notice and discuss main ideas, details, and more. It got my students talking about nonfiction just as enthusiastically as they had been talking about fiction. We were on to something good!

A Book Is Born

Inspired by the overwhelming response the bookmarks received with students, parents, and colleagues, I decided to share these exciting tools in a book. *Reading Response Bookmarks and Graphic Organizers* includes ready-to-copy versions of the fiction and nonfiction bookmarks, plus lesson plans with reproducible graphic organizers to help you make the most of the bookmarks in your classroom. Whether you are having students retell whole stories and texts or exploring specific aspects of a text, such as characters or main idea, you'll find valuable, easy-to-use resources on these pages.

The first lesson for each bookmark offers a way to introduce that bookmark and its images to your class. After that, the order in which you use the lessons and organizers is entirely up to you. You can teach the comprehension lessons in the order in which they are presented, or pick and choose which strategies you want to target first. You can cover all of the fiction strategies before moving on to nonfiction, or hop back and forth between the two genres. And one of the greatest things about the graphic organizers and lessons is that they are designed to be used over and over again. For example, students might complete the Main Characters graphic organizer six or seven times throughout the school year as they enjoy different books. The more often they explore a strategy, the more skilled students will get at retelling and comprehending.

Rooted in Research

The bookmarks and organizers in this book are designed to guide students in retelling important parts of a story or nonfiction text. Over the past two decades, studies have shown that retelling is one of the most effective ways for students to improve comprehension—and for teachers to measure it. Unlike completing multiple-choice or fill-in-the-blank questions, retelling calls on a student to play a very active, personal role in reconstructing the story or text. The student must recall ideas from the text, decide what is most important, and finally, put those ideas in his or her own words and voice. Studies have shown that retelling is an effective comprehension strategy for readers of varying proficiencies and for ESL students as well as native English speakers.

Studies have also uncovered some other interesting instructional benefits of retelling. In addition to boosting comprehension of a specific text, the process of retelling improves a student's sense of story structure and general text organization. This sense is a crucial ingredient to students' success in writing their own stories and essays. And, as you might imagine, retelling a story to classmates also goes a long way toward improving a student's oral language development.

Meeting the Common Core State Standards

Whether your state has its own language arts standards or has adopted the Common Core State Standards, the ideas and activities in this book will help you address those goals. The following is a snapshot of how the bookmarks and lessons support the Common Core State Standards for grades 1 to 3:

READING STANDARDS FOR FICTION

Key Ideas and Details
- Ask and answer key questions about details in a text.
- Retell stories, including key details, and demonstrate understanding of their central message or lesson.
- Describe characters, settings, and major events in a story, using key details; describe how characters respond to major events and challenges.

Craft and Structure
- Describe the overall structure of a story, including describing how the beginning introduces the story and the ending concludes the action.
- Refer to parts of stories, dramas, and poems when writing or speaking about a text, using terms such as chapter, scene, and stanza; describe how each successive part builds on earlier sections.

Integration of Knowledge and Ideas
- Use information gained from the illustrations and words in a print or digital text to demonstrate understanding of its characters, setting, or plot.
- Compare and contrast the adventures and experiences of characters in stories.

Range of Reading and Level of Text Complexity
- Read and comprehend grade-appropriate literature.

READING STANDARDS FOR NONFICTION

Key Ideas and Details

- Ask and answer key questions about details in a text.
- Identify the main topic or main idea of a text; recount key details and explain how they support the main idea.
- Describe the connection between two individuals, events, ideas, or pieces of information in a text.

Craft and Structure

- Know and use various text features (e.g., bold print, headings, etc.) to locate key facts or information in a text.
- Distinguish between information provided by pictures or other illustrations and information provided by the words in a text.
- Identify the main purpose of a text, including what the author wants to answer, explain, or describe. (Introduced in grade 2)
- Distinguish their own point of view from that of the author of a text. (Introduced in grade 3)

Integration of Knowledge and Ideas

- Use the illustrations and details in a text to describe its key ideas.
- Identify the reasons an author gives to support points in a text.
- Identify basic similarities in and differences between two texts on the same topic.
- Describe the logical connection between particular sentences and paragraphs in a text (e.g., comparison, cause/effect, first/second/third in a sequence). (Introduced in grade 3)

Range of Reading and Level of Text Complexity

- Read and comprehend grade-appropriate informational texts, with scaffolding as needed.

Getting Started With Interactive Bookmarks

Inside a "Bookmark Classroom"

In this section, I describe what my "bookmark classroom" looks like in order to help you see the role the bookmarks, lessons, and organizers can play in your own instruction.

The Big Picture

I use the bookmarks with my students in two important ways. One is simply working our way down the bookmark to retell a complete story. This can be a whole-class activity, a small-group activity, or even an activity completed at home with a parent or caregiver. Retellings can begin in the first days of school, although I find that students get better and better at them through the year. The second way I use the bookmarks is to focus attention on a single story element or comprehension strategy. For example, I might call attention to the setting icon on the fiction bookmark and then spend a language arts period exploring setting in a story. The bookmark on its own offers a great way to start talking about these elements, and the reproducible graphic organizers help guide students' thinking.

Timing

Because I want my students to get comfortable talking about their reading right off the bat, I introduce the fiction bookmark in the first few weeks of the school year. See the "Meet the Fiction Bookmark" lesson (page 14) for a great way to introduce it. I focus on fiction for a few months, then begin to incorporate the nonfiction bookmark as well. If you prefer, you can introduce both bookmarks early on and alternate between the two.

Distribution

At first, my students get one bookmark that stays in the classroom. They can color it however they choose and must write their name on the back. Once I am confident that they know how to use the bookmark to retell a story, I give each student a second bookmark for home. (I laminate or use contact paper to make sure both bookmarks will stand up to wear and tear.)

Whole-Class Instruction

In my classroom, bookmark discussions are very often done as a whole class. I frequently read short stories, picture books, and book chapters aloud to the entire class. Then, we all use our bookmarks to practice retelling all or part of the story. (Among my favorite texts to use for this purpose is any installment in Cynthia Rylant's Poppleton series. Each Poppleton book includes several stories, and most are the perfect length for a retelling exercise.) Together, we name the title of the book or story and identify the characters, setting, problem kick-off, and the character's initial feelings. Then, I invite student volunteers to take turns retelling the other important parts of the story (subsequent events, problem wrap-up, and the character's feelings in the end).

Bookmark Partners

Once the whole class has heard a complete retelling, I often have students break into pairs for a second round. With a bookmark in hand, they listen to each other retell the same story in their own words. This offers additional reinforcement and review.

Guided-Reading Groups

I sometimes use the bookmarks in guided-reading groups (four to six students) to hone specific comprehension strategies. For example, I might ask a group that has just finished reading a short chapter book to focus on the two heart images on the bookmark (representing the main character's feelings at the beginning and end of the story). I have found that the bookmarks facilitate these small-group discussions by serving as visual reminders of where the conversation is supposed to be heading. Different groups may be focusing on different comprehension strategies at any given time.

Homework

Once or twice a week, my language arts homework assignment will ask students to use the bookmark to retell a story, chapter, or section to their parents. Usually the child just notes with whom they shared. After a few weeks, I'll ask parents for feedback with a quick query, "How did your child do retelling tonight?" A brief response will let me know that the student is using the bookmark effectively at home. In case parents want to know more about the bookmarks, I have students leave the explanatory chart (see pages 15 and 43) in their homework folders. From time to time, you may choose to assign a graphic organizer for homework as well.

The Writing Connection

Once we have become solid talkers about reading, it's time for the students to learn to write about reading. I often begin with a "free write," where students have an opportunity to write anything they'd like about their reading. I'll start by reading a picture book to the class and have the students respond on a large sticky note. When the responses are in, we sort them and notice that most students write about the characters, problems, etc. Later, when I want to direct students into specific ways of writing, I use reproducible organizers like the ones I share in this book.

I keep copies of the various graphic organizers in a binder with plastic sleeves. As I plan a reading group, I think about what type of response I want students to produce. If I choose to have them write, I'll pick a sheet that supports the teaching purpose. I never expect my students to write every time they read a book. I usually choose a writing moment once or twice a week in school and once or twice a week for homework.

Tips for Teachers

- Laminate the bookmarks to keep them looking good all year long.
- Always keep a stash of extra bookmarks for students who lose theirs.
- When students use the bookmarks to talk about stories and nonfiction texts, remind them to use their own words.
- Remember that if students need to revisit a story to complete a retelling, it is perfectly OK. It's a sign the student is monitoring his or her own comprehension.

Build Your Classroom Library

Fiction Favorites

The following are some short fiction books that lend themselves to strong retellings. Try using them with the lessons and organizers on pages 12–39.

Dog Breath by Dav Pilkey

Goldilocks and the Three Bears (any version)

Good Driving, Amelia Bedelia by Herman Parish and Lynn Sweat

Grandpa Comes to Stay by Rob Lewis

Henry and Mudge books by Cynthia Rylant (any story)

Herbie Jones Sails Into Second Grade by Suzie Kline

Knuffle Bunny by Mo Willems

Mr. Putter and Tabby by Cynthia Rylant

Poppleton and *Poppleton Everyday* by Cynthia Rylant

Recess Queen by Alexis O'Neill and Laura Huliska-Beith

Stand Tall, Molly Lou Melon by Patty Lovell and David Catrow

Stellaluna by Janell Canon

The Three Little Pigs (any version)

When Sophie Gets Angry by Molly Bang

Where the Wild Things Are by Maurice Sendak

Any books by Patricia Polacco

Any books by Tomie dePaola

Jot down the titles of other fiction books you have used successfully for retellings; you may want to use them again in the future.

_____

_____

_____

_____

Nonfiction Favorites

The following are just a few nonfiction books that work well for student retellings. You'll find many more in your school or local library. Use these books with the lessons and organizers on pages 40–63.

All About Lizards by Jim Arnosky

All Pigs Are Beautiful by Dick King Smith (great for identifying facts and opinions)

Born to Be Giants: How Baby Dinosaurs Grew to Rule the World by Lita Judge

Bugs by Rosie Dickins

Castle by David Macaulay

Fly Traps! Plants That Bite Back by Martin Jenkins

I Love Guinea Pigs by Dick King Smith (great for identifying facts and opinions)

Owls by Gail Gibbons

Martin's Big Words: The Life of Dr. Martin Luther King, Jr. by Doreen Rappaport

Spiders by Nic Bishop

What Is a Plant? by Bobby Kalman

Any books in Scholastic's I Can Read nonfiction series

Record the titles of other nonfiction books you have used successfully for retellings so that you can return to them later.

_____

_____

_____

_____

_____

_____

_____

_____

My Fiction Bookmark

Title and author

 Characters

 Setting

Problem kick-off

Feelings of main character (beginning)

First...

Next...

Then...

Problem wrap-up

Feelings of main character (end)

My Fiction Bookmark

Title and author

 Characters

       Setting

Problem kick-off

Feelings of main character (beginning)

First...

Next...

Then...

Problem wrap-up

Feelings of main character (end)

My Fiction Bookmark

Title and author

        Characters

  Setting

Problem kick-off

Feelings of main character (beginning)

First...

Next...

Then...

Problem wrap-up

Feelings of main character (end)

My Fiction Bookmark

Title and author

 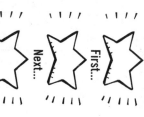          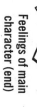 Characters

Setting

Problem kick-off

Feelings of main character (beginning)

First...

Next...

Then...

Problem wrap-up

Feelings of main character (end)

My Fiction Bookmark

Title and author

      Characters

Setting

Problem kick-off

Feelings of main character (beginning)

First...

Next...

Then...

Problem wrap-up

Feelings of main character (end)

My Fiction Bookmark

Title and author

Characters

Setting

Problem kick-off

Feelings of main character (beginning)

First...

Next...

Then...

Problem wrap-up

Feelings of main character (end)

My Fiction Bookmark

 Title and author

 Characters

  Setting

       Problem kick-off

   Feelings of main character (beginning)

First...

Next...

Then...

Problem wrap-up

Feelings of main character (end)

My Fiction Bookmark

 Title and author

 Characters

Setting

  Problem kick-off

  Feelings of main character (beginning)

First...

Next...

Then...

Problem wrap-up

Feelings of main character (end)

My Fiction Bookmark

 Title and author

 Characters

Setting

   Problem kick-off

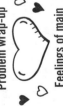 Feelings of main character (beginning)

First...

Next...

Then...

Problem wrap-up

Feelings of main character (end)

My Fiction Bookmark

 Title and author

 Characters

Setting

    Problem kick-off

Feelings of main character (beginning)

First...

Next...

Then...

Problem wrap-up

Feelings of main character (end)

Lesson Page

Meet the Fiction Bookmark

Overview:

Introduce students to the fiction bookmark and its symbols.

Before Using This Organizer:

Choose a picture book to share with the class. (If you prefer, you can use a book the class has already read.) Make copies of pages 12–13 and cut out a bookmark for each student. But do not warm up the laminating machine just yet—your students will enjoy coloring their own bookmarks as part of this lesson! Also make individual student copies of the explanatory chart on page 15. I like to place this reference page in each student's homework folder to remind students and parents of the meanings behind the bookmark symbols.

Directions:

① Distribute the bookmarks and reference charts. Introduce the purpose of using the bookmark. Point out that, like all bookmarks, it can be used to mark a reader's place in a story. But this particular bookmark has another important job: It reminds us of important ideas to think about when we read. Those ideas can help us better understand and remember a story.

② Explain that the pictures on the bookmark are symbols for important parts of a story, and that when students use the bookmark to talk about a book, they can put a finger on the symbol for the part of the story they are describing.

③ Discuss with students what each symbol means and why it is important for readers to think about.

Title and author: Review that these elements are usually found on the cover. Point out that the title can give clues about what will happen in the story. Sometimes knowing the author provides clues, too.

Characters: Review that a story can have many characters, but usually there are one or two main characters. Paying attention to how they think and act can help us understand a story.

Setting: Remind students that the setting is the time and place in which a story happens.

Problem kick-off: Explain that every story has a problem that the main characters try to solve. It is usually introduced near the beginning of a story. The way the problem starts is the "kick-off."

Feelings (in the beginning): This symbol represents how the main character feels in the beginning of the story.

First, Next, and Then: The three star symbols remind students to think about important events in the story's plot. In most stories, the action builds to a really big moment (for example, when the detective figures out the mystery or the lost child spots his mother). The bookmark prompt "Then" can help readers recall this big moment.

Problem wrap-up: At the end of a story, an author tells how the problem gets solved for good.

Feelings (at the end): A character's feelings often change by the end of the story. The change tells us what the character might have learned in the story.

④ Read aloud a picture book, then model using the bookmark to retell important story elements.

Name _____

Meet the Fiction Bookmark

My Fiction Bookmark

Title and author

Characters

Setting

Problem kick-off

Feelings of main character (beginning)

First...

Next...

Then...

Problem wrap-up

Feelings of main character (end)

Point to each part of your bookmark.
Ask yourself these questions:

Title and author: What is the book called? Who wrote it? Can I guess what the book will be about?

Characters: Who are the most important characters?

Setting: When does the story take place? Where does the story take place?

Problem kick-off: What is the problem in the story? How does it start?

Feelings (beginning): How does the main character feel at the beginning of the story?

First: What happens first as the character tries to solve the problem? Does the problem get worse somehow?

Next: What happens next?

Then: What is the most exciting or important thing that happens?

Problem wrap-up: How does the problem end?

Feelings (end): How does the main character feel at the end of the story?

Lesson Page

Make Predictions

Overview:

Students should realize that thinking begins even before a book is opened. In this activity, students will use the title and cover picture to make predictions about a book.

Before Using This Organizer:

Choose a picture book that is new to students and has an interesting title and cover image. Make copies of page 17.

Directions:

1. Hold up your bookmark and touch the book cover symbol. Have students recall which story elements it represents (title and author). Point out that a title helps us start thinking about a story even before we open the book. The title—along with the cover picture—can help us answer: *What will this book be about? Who are the characters? What might the problem be?* Explain that thinking about these questions in advance is a good strategy for understanding what we read. The strategy is called making predictions.

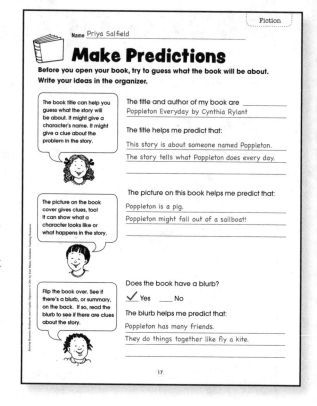

2. Distribute the organizer to students. Explain that the class is going to hear a story and work together to answer the questions on the organizer. Let students know that you will do the writing; students should leave their copies blank.

3. Show students the book cover. Read the title and author's name aloud. Then, read the first prompt on the organizer and ask what students can predict about the story from the title (and author, if applicable). Model recording these predictions on the organizer.

4. Discuss what predictions students can make from the cover picture. Model adding these predictions under the second prompt on the organizer.

5. Tell students that sometimes the back cover of a book has a summary called a blurb. It often has interesting clues about the story. Flip your book over and read aloud the blurb if there is one. Record any clues you find under the last prompt.

6. Read the book and discuss whether students' predictions were on target.

7. Have students choose a book they have never read before from the classroom library. Ask them to fill in their own copies of the organizer before they open the book.

Bookmark Connections

When students make predictions, have them touch the book cover image.

Name _____

Make Predictions

Before you open your book, try to guess what the book will be about. Write your ideas in the organizer.

The book title can help you guess what the story will be about. It might give a character's name. It might give a clue about the problem in the story.

The picture on the book cover gives clues, too! It can show what a character looks like or what happens in the story.

Flip the book over. See if there's a blurb, or summary, on the back. If so, read the blurb to see if there are clues about the story.

The title and author of my book are _____

_____

The title helps me predict that:

_____

_____

_____

The picture on this book helps me predict that:

_____

_____

_____

Does the book have a blurb?

____ Yes   ____ No

The blurb helps me predict that:

_____

_____

Lesson Page
Retell a Story

Overview:
Students will retell the important components of a story.

Before Using This Organizer:
Review the meanings of the symbols on the bookmark. Make copies of page 19 for students to complete.

Directions:

1. Have students read a short, level-appropriate fiction book like the ones listed on page 10. Each student can read and retell a different story from your classroom library. If you prefer all students to work with the same tale, read a story aloud to the class or use an engaging story from your reading program.

2. Remind students to refer to the bookmark as they read or listen. Review that touching each image as they read can remind them to pay attention to the title, characters, setting, plot problem, and so on.

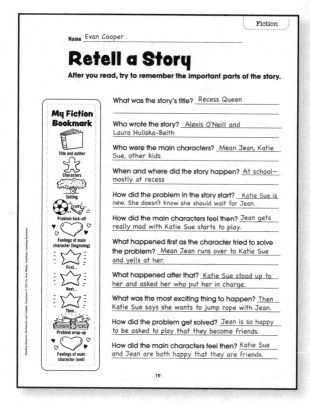

3. After reading, ask student volunteers to retell their stories using the images on the bookmark. Students can stand and model touching the images on the bookmark as they report to the class.

4. Distribute the graphic organizer on page 19 and have students record their retellings on the sheet.

5. Have students complete the organizer for other fiction books throughout the year.

Bookmark Connections

When students retell a story, have them touch all of the bookmark images in sequence. While one student retells, have each student in the group hold his or her own bookmark and move a finger down the bookmark. If the reteller gets stuck, ask another child to take over from that point.

Name _____

Retell a Story

After you read, try to remember the important parts of the story.

My Fiction Bookmark

Title and author

Characters

Setting

Problem kick-off

Feelings of main character (beginning)

First...

Next...

Then...

Problem wrap-up

Feelings of main character (end)

What was the story's title? _____
_____

Who wrote the story? _____
_____

Who were the main characters? _____
_____

When and where did the story happen? _____
_____

How did the problem in the story start? _____
_____

How did the main characters feel then? _____
_____

What happened first as the character tried to solve the problem? _____
_____

What happened after that? _____
_____

What was the most exciting thing to happen? _____
_____

How did the problem get solved? _____
_____

How did the main characters feel then? _____
_____

Lesson Page

What a Character!

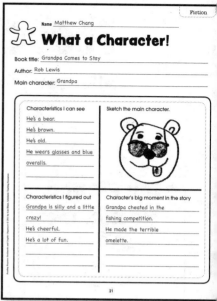

Overview:

Conversations around stories become richer when students are taught ways to think about characters. Here, students will use internal and external traits to describe a character from a story.

Before Using This Organizer:

Have a T-chart ready (on chart paper, the chalkboard, or interactive whiteboard) on which you have written the headings "External Traits" and "Internal Traits." Choose a picture book that includes a well-developed character. Make copies of page 21 for students to complete.

Directions:

1. Read aloud a book. Model identifying a trait that readers can tell about the character just by looking at the pictures (such as gender or hair color). Ask students what else the pictures tell about the character.

2. Introduce the T-chart. Point to the heading "External Traits" and explain that external traits are things that we can see or observe. Guide students to notice that all of the traits you have discussed so far are external traits, and record these traits on the T-chart.

3. Explain that authors often use words to tell us about a character's external traits. He or she might include descriptions such as:

   Grayson was a shaggy dog.
   Bethany pushed her glasses up.

   Phrases like "shaggy" and "glasses" tell us what we would see if we could look at the character. Help students recall similar examples from your book. Record them on your T-chart.

4. Explain that characters have internal traits, too. These are things that readers can't know just by looking at the character. Instead, these traits describe the character's personality. Explain that readers usually have to figure out (or "infer") a character's internal traits from the way the character acts or speaks. Discuss an example or two, such as:

   Olivia stood up to a bully. We can guess that she is _____. (brave)

5. Model using clues in the story to name an internal trait of the character you are exploring. Invite students to describe others. Add these traits to the "Internal Traits" side of your T-chart.

6. Distribute the organizer and review the directions. Have students independently complete the sheet for a character from a favorite book.

Bookmark Connections

When students use the bookmark to talk about characters, have them describe each character's traits and their importance to the story.

Name _____

What a Character!

Book title: _____

Author: _____

Main character: _____

Characteristics I can see	Sketch the main character.
_____ _____ _____ _____ _____	
Characteristics I figured out	**Character's big moment in the story**
_____ _____ _____ _____	_____ _____ _____ _____

Lesson Page
Compare Characters

Overview:
Students will compare and contrast story characters using a Venn diagram.

Before Using This Organizer:
Decide whether you would like to have students compare characters from the same story or two different stories. Choose read-aloud books accordingly. Make copies of page 23.

Directions:
① Draw a Venn diagram on the board or whiteboard and review how it works. Use the diagram to help students compare and contrast two everyday items—

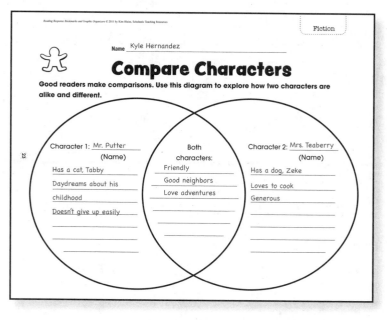

Name __Kyle Hernandez__

Compare Characters

Good readers make comparisons. Use this diagram to explore how two characters are alike and different.

Character 1: Mr. Putter
(Name)
Has a cat, Tabby
Daydreams about his childhood
Doesn't give up easily

Both characters:
Friendly
Good neighbors
Love adventures

Character 2: Mrs. Teaberry
(Name)
Has a dog, Zeke
Loves to cook
Generous

apples and oranges, for example. Emphasize that similarities between the two items belong in the middle, where the two circles overlap. A statement that describes only one of the items belongs on that item's side of the diagram.

② Explain that students will use a Venn diagram to compare two characters. If students are unfamiliar with the characters you have chosen, introduce the characters to the class.

③ Read aloud the story or stories in which the two characters appear.

④ Distribute the graphic organizer and have students begin by recording the names of the two characters. Draw a blank Venn diagram on the board so that you can model the process of completing the diagram.

⑤ Elicit what students know about each character. As students name a character trait, ask if the trait describes character 1, character 2, or both. Model recording each trait in the appropriate spot, and have students record it on their papers.

⑥ Encourage students to include statements about the character's role in the story. Examples of such statements that could appear in the diagram include:

Goes on an adventure

Tries to solve a problem

Has a disagreement

Is happy at the end of the story

Bookmark Connections

As students compare characters, they can put their fingers on the character and feelings symbols on the bookmark.

Name _____

Compare Characters

Good readers make comparisons. Use this diagram to explore how two characters are alike and different.

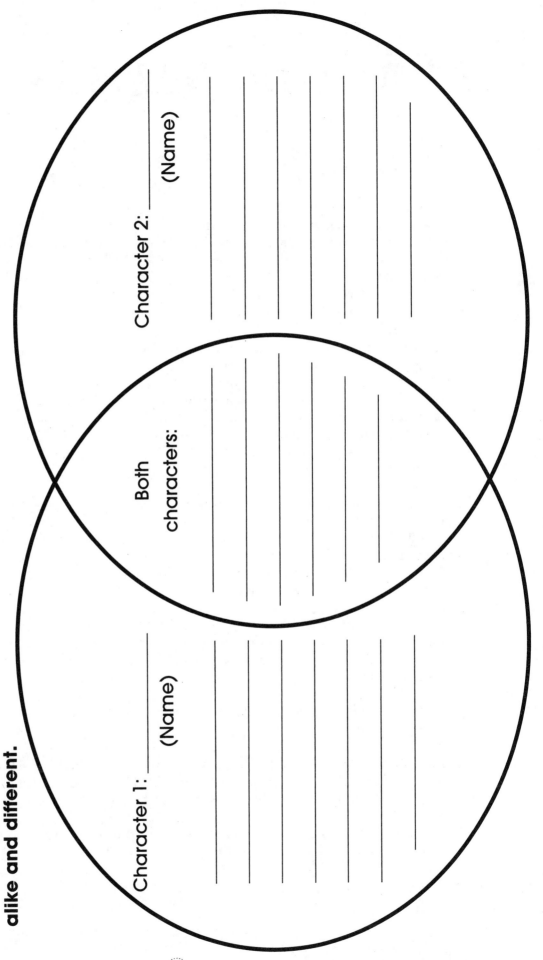

Character 2: _____
(Name)

Both characters:

Character 1: _____
(Name)

Lesson Page

Describe the Setting

Overview:
Students will learn to identify and describe the setting (place and time) of a story.

Before Using This Organizer:
Choose a familiar book that takes place in an identifiable setting. Big Books and books available for viewing on an interactive whiteboard are ideal, since students will be looking at pictures for clues about the setting. Make copies of page 25.

Directions:
1. Explain that the setting is where and when a story takes place. Ask students to brainstorm examples of where a story can happen (school, a character's home, etc.). Then ask for examples of when a story can happen. For early readers, I usually keep this aspect of setting simple, referring to time periods as "long ago," "present time," or "in the future."

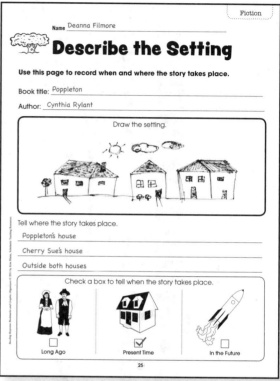

2. Talk about how readers know the setting. In some books, the author tells us the time and place. In other books, we look for clues in the pictures or story. For example, when I read the story *Poppleton* with my class, I point out that Cherry Sue calls Poppleton on the telephone. This helps us decide that the story takes place in modern times or "today." We can also guess from the pictures that much of the story takes place at Poppleton's house.

3. Read aloud the book you have chosen and model listing the setting locations (some stories have more than one). Discuss how you identified the setting. Was it named? Described? Shown in pictures? Guide students to notice words that indicate setting, like *inside*, *upstairs*, and so on.

4. Work with students to identify the time period of the text. Discuss ways the author revealed the time period.

5. Have students work with a partner or independently to search for setting descriptions and clues in an appropriately leveled book. Distribute the graphic organizer and have them record the setting.

6. Discuss students' findings and look for patterns. Did some settings appear in several books? Was one time period most common?

Bookmark Connections

When students talk about setting, have them touch the tree symbol on the bookmark.

Name _____

Describe the Setting

Use this page to record when and where the story takes place.

Book title: _____

Author: _____

> Draw the setting.
>
>
>
>
>
>
>
>

Tell where the story takes place.

_____

_____

Check a box to tell when the story takes place.

☐

Long Ago

☐

Present Time

☐

In the Future

25

Lesson Page
Find the Problem

Overview:
Every story has a problem. Here, students will identify the problem that "kicks off" a story.

Before Using This Organizer:
Have on hand a familiar, grade-appropriate book with an interesting plot problem. Make copies of page 27.

Directions:

1. Explain to students that every story has a problem. It is usually introduced near the beginning of the story. Things really get fun when the characters react to the problem and try to solve it! Have students recall the problems in some books they have read. Do they remember how each problem started? Remind students that the soccer ball picture on the fiction bookmark asks them to recall the way a problem starts.

2. Hold up the book you selected for today's lesson. Invite students to recall the problem in the story. If necessary, read the story aloud until you come to the introduction of the problem. Write this problem "kick-off" on the board or whiteboard.

3. Ask students to recall how the main character feels about the problem at the beginning of the story. Read aloud bits of the story that might help them infer the character's feelings. Record the feelings on the board or whiteboard. Remind students that the first heart on the fiction bookmark asks them to describe the character's feelings about the problem.

4. Invite students to talk about how they would handle the problem if they were the main character.

5. Distribute copies of the graphic organizer and model filling it in for the book you just discussed.

6. Instruct students to use their own copies of the sheet to record the problem kick-off and the character's feelings from their independent reading books.

Teaching Tip:
When your students are working with a reading partner, provide time for them to discuss their thoughts before using the organizer.

Bookmark Connections

When students describe the kick-off, have them touch the soccer ball image on the bookmark.

Name _____

 # Find the Problem

Use this page to identify the problem that happens in your story.

Book title: _____

Author: _____

> Draw the problem in the story.

Tell how the problem starts, or kicks off.

_____

_____

Tell how the main character feels about the problem.	Tell how YOU would handle the problem if you were the main character.
_____	_____
_____	_____
_____	_____
_____	_____

Lesson Page

What Happened?

Overview:

Students will learn to retell the main events of a story in chronological order. (Because this skill can be challenging for young readers, the graphic organizer has been modified for three levels. Organizer 1, on page 29, has students retell main events in words. Organizer 2, on page 30, lets struggling students draw the main events. Organizer 3, on page 31, has students retell main events using both words and pictures and is a good intermediary step.)

Before Using This Organizer:

Choose a familiar book with a clear sequence of events. Decide whether your students will be most successful recounting main events in words, pictures, or a combination of the two. Make copies of the appropriate version of the graphic organizer.

Directions:

1. Remind students that the star symbols on the bookmark help us remember important events from a story. Point out that words like *first*, *next*, and *then* help us retell those events in order.

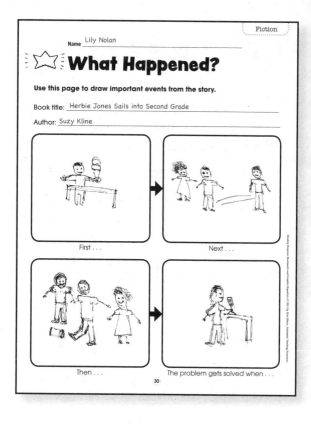

2. Hold up the book you have chosen. Ask students to recall the problem in the book. Ask: *After we find out about the problem, what happens first? What happens after that?*

3. Have students recount the main events in order, revisiting the story if necessary. List the events on the board or whiteboard using time-order words. Guide students to focus on events that are important to the story. These events usually show how the problem gets worse or how the characters try to solve the problem.

4. Using the word *then*, help students identify the most exciting or important event in the book. (In the older grades, students will learn that this is the "climax" of the book.) In one book, it might be the scene when the detective gets the final clue. In another, it might be the last round in an intense spelling bee.

5. Have students recall the way the problem is solved or "wrapped up." Record this on the board or whiteboard.

6. Discuss what students thought of the story and record a few comments.

7. Distribute the graphic organizers and have students record important plot events from their independent reading books.

Bookmark Connections

Have students touch the star symbols as they name the story's main events and the wrapped gift symbol as they describe the "wrap-up," or solution.

Name _____

 # What Happened?

Use this page to write about important events from the story.

Book title: _____

Author: _____

☆ First,

_____

_____

☆ Next,

_____

_____

☆ Then,

_____

_____

🎁 Wrap-Up

The problem gets solved when:

_____

_____

_____

29

Name _____

⭐ What Happened?

Use this page to draw important events from the story.

Book title: _____

Author: _____

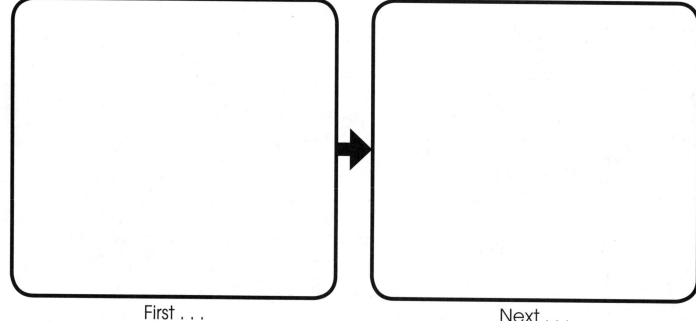

First . . .   Next . . .

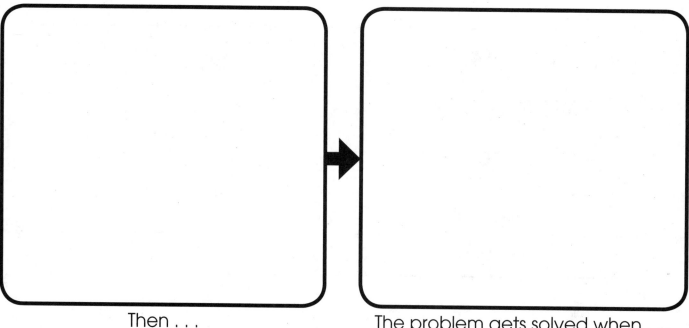

Then . . .   The problem gets solved when . . .

Name _____

What Happened?

Use this page to draw and write about important events from the story.

Book title: _____

Author: _____

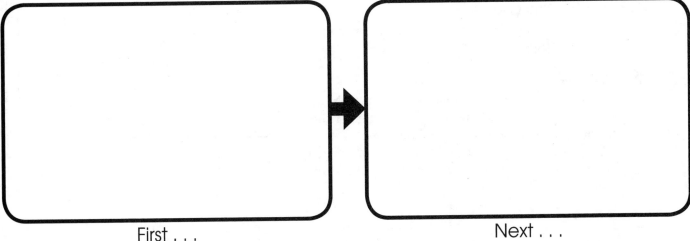

First . . .   Next . . .

_____   _____

_____   _____

Then . . .   The problem gets solved when . . .

_____   _____

_____   _____

Lesson Page
Cause and Effect

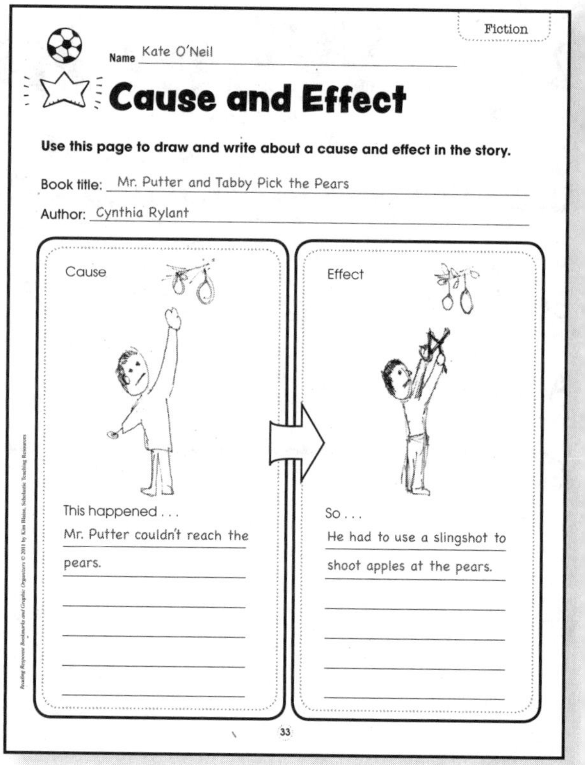

Overview:
Students sometimes struggle to recognize the causal connection between events in a story. In this lesson, they will use the events in a story to identify cause and effect.

Before Using This Organizer:
Choose a short fiction book with a clear plot sequence to share with students. Make copies of page 33.

Directions:
① Demonstrate a physical cause and effect. Hold up a pencil and point out that when you let go of the pencil, it falls to the floor. Here, the cause is letting go of the pencil, and the effect is the pencil falling. Ask students to name the possible effects of other causes:

Cause	Effect
It's raining at lunchtime…	so we can't go out for recess.
Dan left his homework at school…	so he couldn't complete it.

② Explain that we see causes and effects in stories, too. This is a common way that a story plot develops. It is often what ties together the events in a story.

③ Distribute the graphic organizer, then read aloud a fiction picture book.

④ After reading, work together to identify the cause of the problem in the story (this is typically the kick-off, or introduction of the problem). Have students describe and draw this cause on the graphic organizer.

⑤ Have students work independently to identify one effect of the cause you identified as a class. Have them describe and draw this effect on the organizer.

Worksheet (page 33):

Fiction

Name _Kate O'Neil_

Cause and Effect

Use this page to draw and write about a cause and effect in the story.

Book title: _Mr. Putter and Tabby Pick the Pears_

Author: _Cynthia Rylant_

Cause

This happened . . .
Mr. Putter couldn't reach the pears.

Effect

So . . .
He had to use a slingshot to shoot apples at the pears.

33

Bookmark Connections

Have students touch the soccer ball and first star on the bookmark when they describe a cause and effect that leads into a story.

Name _____

Cause and Effect

Use this page to draw and write about a cause and effect in the story.

Book title: _____

Author: _____

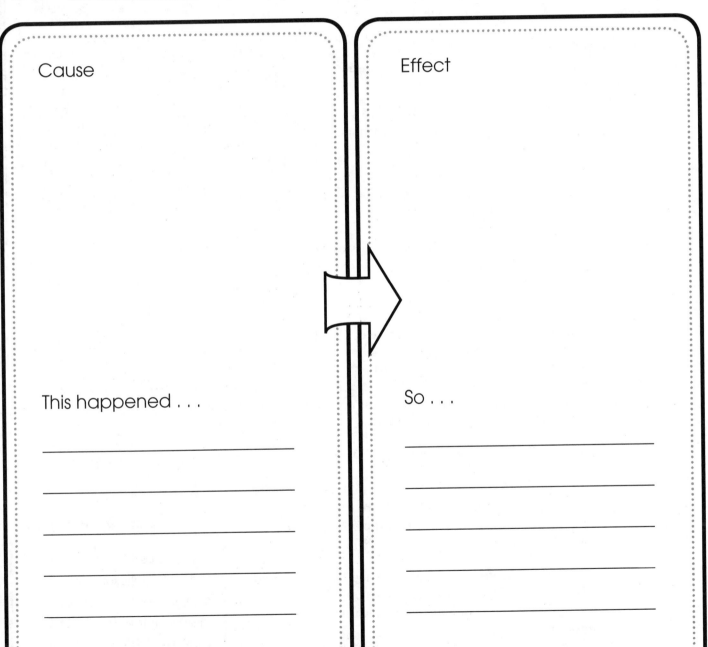

Cause

Effect

This happened . . .

So . . .

_____

_____

_____

_____

_____

_____

_____

_____

_____

_____

Lesson Page

Solving the Problem

Overview:
Students will identify the problem and solution in a story and identify the main character's feelings about the solution.

Before Using This Organizer:
Identify the problem and solution together each time you read aloud. For this lesson, choose a short fiction book to share. Make copies of page 35.

Directions:
1. Introduce problem and solution with real-life examples. For example:

Problem:	Possible Solution:
It is too warm in classroom…	We open our window.
I don't understand a math problem…	I ask the teacher for help.

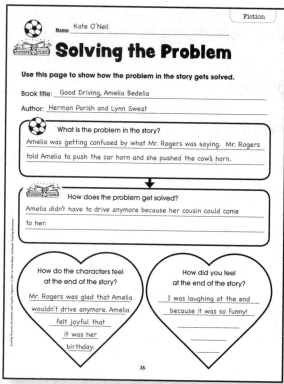

1. Remind students that we see problems in stories as well as in real life. The events in the story often show how the characters try to solve their problem. The ending of the story usually describes the solution.

2. Distribute the graphic organizer, then read aloud a short fiction book. Work with students to identify the main problem in the book.

6. Have students name the solution to the problem described in the story. Point out that the main character may have tried many different ways to solve the problem. Have students name the solution that works in the end.

4. On the organizer, have students draw and describe both the problem and the solution.

5. Ask students to think about how the main characters feel about the way the problem is solved. Have them describe each character's feelings at the end of the book on the graphic organizer.

6. Invite students to think about their own feelings at the end of the book and to describe those feelings on the graphic organizer. They can use the box of "feelings" words on the page as a guide.

Bookmark Connections

As you discuss the problem, have students touch the soccer ball image. As you discuss the solution, have students touch the wrapped gift. As you discuss the characters' feelings, have students touch the second heart.

Name _____

Solving the Problem

Use this page to show how the problem in the story gets solved.

Book title: _____

Author: _____

What is the problem in the story?

_____

_____

How does the problem get solved?

_____

_____

How do the characters feel
at the end of the story?

_____

_____

_____

_____

How did you feel
at the end of the story?

_____

_____

_____

_____

Lesson Page

What's the Message?

Overview:

Students will learn to identify the message or theme of a story by considering what the main character learned.

Before Using This Organizer:

Discussing the message or lesson inherent in each read-aloud book you share will provide the practice needed for independent work. For this lesson, choose a fiction story with a clear moral, message, or theme. Make copies of page 37.

Directions:

① Remind students of the problems and solutions in some familiar stories. In each case, ask students to think about what the main character learned in the story. For example, in the fairy tale *Goldilocks and the Three Bears*, Goldilocks learns that she should have respected the bears' property. Point out that this lesson is sometimes called the theme or message of the story. It is a lesson that readers can learn along with the main character.

② Tell students that you are going to read aloud a story, then work together to find the message. Read the story you have chosen.

③ Distribute the graphic organizer and instruct students to start by recording the problem and solution. Then, discuss what lesson the main character learned. Have students write a sentence describing that lesson on the organizer.

④ Invite students to think about how they can apply the same lesson to their own lives. Have them write their response in the last section of the organizer. Note that similar language can be used to describe what the characters learned and what message readers can take from the story.

Teaching Tip:

It can be helpful to prepare some possible messages and let students choose which one matches the story. Some messages common in children's literature are:

The importance of honesty

The importance of being a good friend

The importance of asking for help when you need it

The importance of hard work

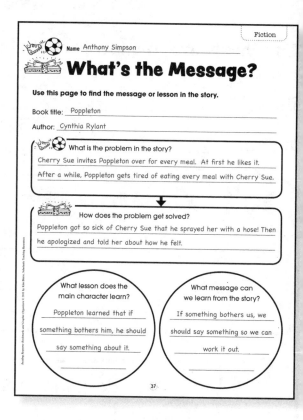

Fiction

Name Anthony Simpson

What's the Message?

Use this page to find the message or lesson in the story.

Book title: Poppleton

Author: Cynthia Rylant

What is the problem in the story?
Cherry Sue invites Poppleton over for every meal. At first he likes it. After a while, Poppleton gets tired of eating every meal with Cherry Sue.

How does the problem get solved?
Poppleton got so sick of Cherry Sue that he sprayed her with a hose! Then he apologized and told her about how he felt.

What lesson does the main character learn?
Poppleton learned that if something bothers him, he should say something about it.

What message can we learn from the story?
If something bothers us, we should say something so we can work it out.

37

Bookmark Connections

Encourage students to include the theme or message when they touch the wrap-up icon and describe the wrap-up of a story.

Name _____

What's the Message?

Use this page to find the message or lesson in the story.

Book title: _____

Author: _____

What is the problem in the story?

_____

_____

How does the problem get solved?

_____

_____

What lesson does the main character learn?

_____

_____

_____

What message can we learn from the story?

_____

_____

_____

Lesson Page

Author Study

Students will notice and describe similarities among texts by the same author. This is an important step in identifying an author's style.

Before Using This Organizer:

This lesson works best as a culminating activity after reading and talking about several books by the same author. Choose two or three books by the same author that your class has enjoyed this year, and have them on hand for this activity. Make copies of page 39.

Directions:

① Ask students to name a favorite author. Then ask if they think they would be able to recognize a story by that author if they read or heard it without seeing the author's name. If so, what clues would help them? For example, does the author always use the same characters? Does he or she always write outdoor adventure stories?

② Explain that students are going to make a chart describing two books by the same author. Then they are going to look for ways that those two books are similar to or different from one another.

③ Remind students of the books you have decided to use for the lesson. If it's been a while since you shared them with the class, allow time for a quick read-aloud.

④ Distribute the graphic organizer. Have students recall the title, characters, problem, and message for the first book and record these elements on the chart. Repeat for the remaining book.

⑤ Ask students to look for and describe some ways the books are different from one another. Then ask them to look for and describe ways the books are similar. Record one similarity on the organizer. Explain that patterns in the way an author writes are called the author's "style."

⑥ Later in the year, have students work in pairs to complete the organizer again for two other books by the same author.

Teaching Tip:

Try creating this chart using a big pocket chart and large index cards.

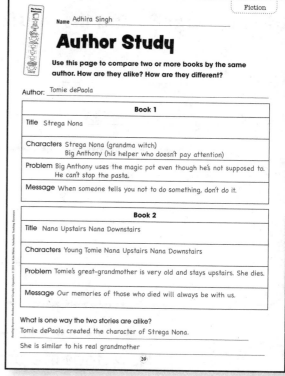

Bookmark Connections

When comparing stories for the chart, students can touch the title, character, kick-off, and wrap-up pictures on the fiction bookmark.

Name _____

Author Study

Use this page to compare two or more books by the same author. How are they alike? How are they different?

Author: _____

Book 1
Title
Characters
Problem
Message

Book 2
Title
Characters
Problem
Message

What is one way the two stories are alike?

_____

_____

My Nonfiction Bookmark

Title and author

Topic of chapter, section, or page

Fact

Fact

Fact

Main idea

Now I wonder...

My Nonfiction Bookmark

Title and author

Topic of chapter, section, or page

Fact

Fact

Fact

Main idea

Now I wonder...

My Nonfiction Bookmark

Title and author

Topic of chapter, section, or page

Fact

Fact

Fact

Main idea

Now I wonder...

My Nonfiction Bookmark

Title and author

Topic of chapter, section, or page

Fact

Fact

Fact

Main idea

Now I wonder...

My Nonfiction Bookmark

Title and author

Topic of chapter, section, or page

Fact

Fact

Fact

Main idea

Now I wonder...

My Nonfiction Bookmark

Title and author

Topic of chapter, section, or page

Fact

Fact

Fact

Main idea

Now I wonder...

My Nonfiction Bookmark

Title and author

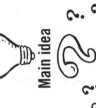

Topic of chapter, section, or page

 Fact

 Fact

 Fact

 Main idea

 Now I wonder...

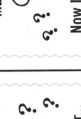

My Nonfiction Bookmark

Title and author

Topic of chapter, section, or page

 Fact

 Fact

 Fact

 Main idea

 Now I wonder...

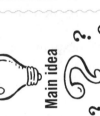

My Nonfiction Bookmark

Title and author

Topic of chapter, section, or page

 Fact

 Fact

 Fact

 Main idea

 Now I wonder...

My Nonfiction Bookmark

Title and author

Topic of chapter, section, or page

 Fact

 Fact

 Fact

 Main idea

 Now I wonder...

My Nonfiction Bookmark

Title and author

Topic of chapter, section, or page

Fact

Fact

Fact

Main idea

Now I wonder...

My Nonfiction Bookmark

Title and author

Topic of chapter, section, or page

Fact

Fact

Fact

Main idea

Now I wonder...

Lesson Page

Meet the Nonfiction Bookmark

Overview:

Introduce students to the nonfiction bookmark and its symbols.

Before Using This Organizer:

Choose a nonfiction book to share with the class. (If the book is long, you may wish to select one chapter or section.) Make copies of pages 40–41 and cut out a bookmark for each student. Also make individual student copies of the explanatory chart on page 43. One can be placed in each student's homework folder to remind students and parents of the meanings behind the bookmark symbols.

Directions:

① Distribute the bookmarks and reference charts. Introduce the purpose of using the bookmark. Point out that, like the fiction bookmark, it reminds us of important ideas to think about when we read. This bookmark reminds us of things to think about when we read nonfiction, or fact-based, books.

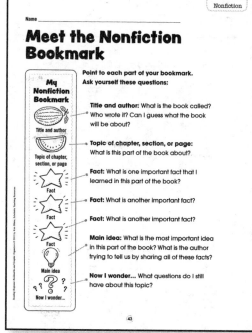

② Explain that the pictures on the bookmark are symbols for important parts of a nonfiction book. Remind students that when they use the bookmark to talk about a book, they can put a finger on the symbol for the part of the book they are describing.

③ Ask students what each symbol means and why it might be important for readers to think about.

Title and author: Review that these elements are usually found on the cover. Point out that the title usually describes what the book is mainly about. The title is like a whole watermelon because it sums up the whole book.

Topic of chapter, section, or page: Review that while a nonfiction book may cover a broad topic, individual pages, sections, or chapters usually focus on smaller, specific topics. Each chapter, section, or page is like a piece of the watermelon.

Facts: Remind students that facts are statements that can be proven true. They tell more about the topic.

Main idea: Explain that the main idea of a page, section, or chapter is a statement that sums up what the text is mostly about. It is the most important idea in the text, and the details all connect to it.

Now I wonder...: This symbol represents questions that readers may have after reading the page, section, or chapter.

④ Read aloud a page, section, or chapter of a grade-appropriate nonfiction book. Model using the bookmark to retell the important nonfiction elements.

Name _____

Meet the Nonfiction Bookmark

My Nonfiction Bookmark

Title and author

Topic of chapter, section, or page

Fact

Fact

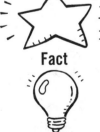

Fact

Main idea

Now I wonder...

Point to each part of your bookmark. Ask yourself these questions:

Title and author: What is the book called? Who wrote it? Can I guess what the book will be about?

Topic of chapter, section, or page: What is this part of the book about?

Fact: What is one important fact that I learned in this part of the book?

Fact: What is another important fact?

Fact: What is another important fact?

Main idea: What is the most important idea in this part of the book? What is the author trying to tell us by sharing all of these facts?

Now I wonder... What questions do I still have about this topic?

Lesson Page
Make Predictions

Overview:
Many students skip the title and headings when reading nonfiction text. Here, students will learn to use these essential text features to make predictions before reading. After reading, they'll revisit their predictions to check for accuracy.

Before Using This Organizer:
Choose a nonfiction text to share with the class. Look for one that has a clear title and includes section or chapter headings. Choose one section to focus on in this lesson. Make copies of page 45.

Directions:

1. Hold up your bookmark and touch the whole watermelon symbol. Have students recall what this symbol represents (the title and author of the whole book). Point out that the title helps us identify what a book will be about.

2. Point out that inside a book, there are often smaller headings or subtitles to introduce each section, page, or chapter. Explain that these headings can also help readers make predictions about the content.

3. Distribute the organizer to students. Explain that the class is going to work together to make predictions about a text.

4. Show students the book cover. Read the title and author's name aloud and have students record these elements on the organizer. Then, read the first prompt on the organizer and ask what students can predict about the text from the title. Guide students to record two predictions on the organizer.

5. Open the book to the page, section, or chapter you have selected. Draw students' attention to any headings or subtitles, and read them aloud. Have students record one heading on the organizer. Invite them to make and record two predictions about this section of text based on the heading.

6. Read the page, section, or chapter aloud. Afterward, discuss whether the class's predictions were on target. Work with students to complete the last section of the organizer accordingly.

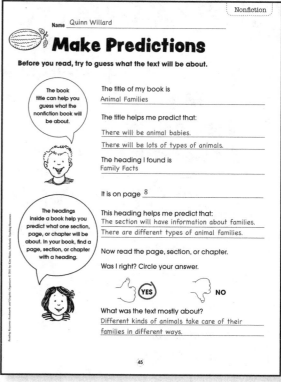

Bookmark Connections

When students make predictions, have them touch the whole watermelon image on the bookmark.

Name _____

Make Predictions

Before you read, try to guess what the text will be about.

> The book title can help you guess what the nonfiction book will be about.

The title of my book is

_____

The title helps me predict that:

_____

_____

The heading I found is

_____

It is on page _____

This heading helps me predict that:

_____

_____

> The headings inside a book help you predict what one section, page, or chapter will be about. In your book, find a page, section, or chapter with a heading.

Now read the page, section, or chapter.

Was I right? Circle your answer.

 YES   **NO**

What was the text mostly about?

_____

_____

Lesson Page

Get Ready to Read

Overview:
Students often have a wealth of information about nonfiction topics. In this lesson, they will learn to tap into their prior knowledge and build on what they already know.

Before Using This Organizer:
Choose a grade-appropriate nonfiction text to share with the class. For this lesson, a short book that can easily be read in one sitting is best. Make copies of page 47.

Directions:
① Physically demonstrate the idea of accessing prior knowledge by opening a drawer in a file cabinet or desk and removing a file. Explain that good readers do something like this each time they read nonfiction text. They know that they have information in their brains that might help them understand the text, and they deliberately recall that information before they start to read.

② Distribute the graphic organizer and have students record the title and author of the book you are going to read. Work together to identify the main topic of the book.

③ Ask students what they already know about this topic. Remind them that they need to tap into this information, just as you took your file out of your desk. Have students record what they already know on the graphic organizer.

④ Have students record on the organizer some ideas they would like to find out about the topic.

⑤ Read the nonfiction book aloud to students. After reading, have students fill in the final part of the organizer with new facts that they learned. Have them reread the list of ideas they wanted to learn about and put a check mark next to any questions that were answered.

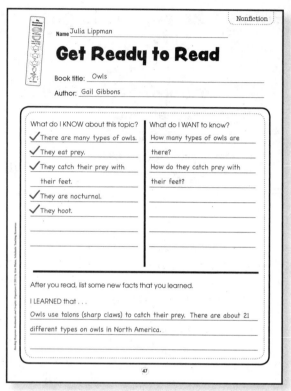

Bookmark Connections

Have students touch the whole watermelon when they name the title of the book and talk about what they already know. Have them touch the question mark when they describe what they want to know and the stars when they share newly acquired facts.

Name _____

Get Ready to Read

Book title: _____

Author: _____

What do I KNOW about this topic?	What do I WANT to know?
_____	_____
_____	_____
_____	_____
_____	_____
_____	_____
_____	_____
_____	_____
_____	_____

After you read, list some new facts that you learned.

I LEARNED that . . .

_____

_____

_____

Lesson Page

Retell a Page or Section

Overview:
Students will retell the important components of a nonfiction page or section.

Before Using This Organizer:
Review the meanings of the symbols on the bookmark. Make copies of page 49 for students to complete.

Directions:

① Have each student read a short, level-appropriate nonfiction book like the ones listed on page 11. Each student can read and retell a portion of a different nonfiction book from your classroom library. If you prefer all students to work with the same text, read a section aloud to the class or use a nonfiction passage from your reading program.

② Remind students to refer to the bookmark as they read or listen. Review that touching each image as they read can help them remember to pay attention to the title, section headings, main ideas, important details, and so on.

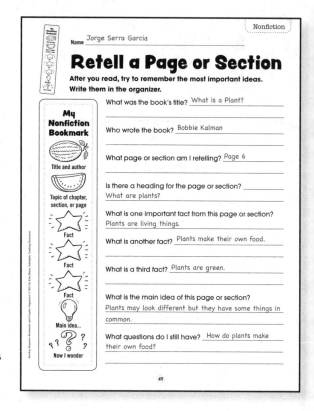

③ After reading, ask student volunteers to retell their sections using the images on the bookmark. Students can stand and model touching the images on the bookmark as they report to the class.

④ Distribute the graphic organizer on page 49 and have students record their retellings on the sheet.

Teaching Tip:
Practice retelling pages as frequently as possible. If I have a student teacher or aide in the room, I often break into two groups to give students more opportunities to retell.

Bookmark Connections

When students retell a page or section, have them touch all of the bookmark images in sequence. While one student retells, have each student in the group hold his or her own bookmark and move a finger down the bookmark. If the reteller gets stuck, ask another child to take over from that point.

Name _____

Retell a Page or Section

After you read, try to remember the most important ideas.

My Nonfiction Bookmark

Title and author

Topic of chapter, section, or page

Fact

Fact

Fact

Main idea

Now I wonder...

What was the book's title? _____

_____

Who wrote the book? _____

_____

What page or section am I retelling? _____

_____

Is there a heading for the page or section? _____

_____

What is one important fact from this page or section?

_____

What is another fact? _____

_____

What is a third fact? _____

_____

What is the main idea of this page or section?

_____

_____

What questions do I still have? _____

_____

_____

Lesson Page

Find the Facts

Overview:
This activity helps students learn to distinguish between facts and opinions in nonfiction texts.

Before Using This Organizer:
Make copies of page 51 for students to complete. Choose a nonfiction book that includes clear statements of opinion (see page 11 for some suggestions).

Directions:

1. Introduce or review the definitions of *fact* and *opinion*. Guide students to understand that a fact is a statement that can be proved true. An opinion is a statement that shows how a person thinks or feels about a topic. It cannot be proved true. Offer some sample statements, and have students identify them as facts or opinions:

   Today is Friday. (fact)
   Friday is the best day of the week.
   (opinion)

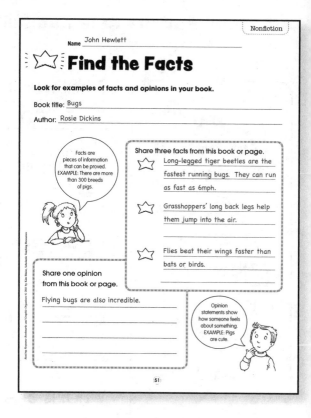

2. Distribute the graphic organizer and have students record the title and author of the nonfiction book you've selected. Read aloud the book (or a section or chapter).

3. Work together to identify one fact from the read-aloud. Have students record it on the organizer. Have students work independently to identify two additional facts and record them on the organizer.

4. Ask students to think of a statement that gave the author's opinion or feelings about the topic. If they have trouble, explain that words like *best, worst, most, least, should*, and *should not* often signal opinion statements. Once students have identified an opinion from the text, have them record it on the organizer. Note that you can do this activity with a book that does not include opinion statements; students can simply write "No opinions found" in that section of the organizer.

Bookmark Connections

Have students touch the watermelon when they name the title of the book. Have them touch the stars when they name facts.

Name _____

Find the Facts

Look for examples of facts and opinions in your book.

Book title: _____

Author: _____

Facts are pieces of information that can be proved. EXAMPLE: There are more than 300 breeds of pigs.

Share three facts from this book or page.

☆ _____
_____
_____

☆ _____
_____
_____

☆ _____
_____
_____

Share one opinion from this book or page.

_____
_____
_____
_____

Opinion statements show how someone feels about something. EXAMPLE: Pigs are cute.

Lesson Page

Using My Own Words

Overview:

True comprehension is evident when a child can restate the facts from a text in his or her own words. This activity will help you teach this difficult but important skill.

Before Using This Organizer:

Make copies of page 53 for students to complete. Choose a nonfiction book to share.

Directions:

① Explain that when we tell other people about a book in a summary, report, or conversation, it is important to put ideas in our own words. When we use the author's exact words as if they are our own, it is a form of stealing.

② Distribute the graphic organizer and review the directions. Explain that it will give students practice in putting ideas from books in their own words. Show students the book you have selected for today and have them record the title and author.

Nonfiction

Name _Juliana Reese_

⭐ Using My Own Words

Try putting ideas from a book in your own words!

Book title: Spiders

Author: Nic Bishop

Copy one fact from this page or book.

⭐ The green lynx spider is perfectly camouflaged when it hides among leaves waiting to pounce on an insect.

Who is the author of that fact?
Nic Bishop
(the book's author)

When I find a fact in a book, it belongs to that book's author. I want to remember the facts in my own words.

Now rewrite that fact using your own words.

⭐ The green lynx spider is green and hides itself in green leaves so it can attack its prey.

It's hard to write facts in my own words. I look away from the book and ask myself what the author is trying to say.

53

---

③ Read aloud the book (or a section from it). Have students identify a fact from the text and copy it word for word in the first section of the organizer. Remind students that those are the author's words.

④ Now have students think of other ways to express the same idea. Have them rewrite the fact in their own words in the second section of the organizer.

⑤ Have students share their rephrasings with the class. Point out how many different ways students found to say the same thing!

Teaching Tip:

This activity works very well in small groups. When a guided-reading group has read the same nonfiction text, try finding facts and restating them. This lesson will pay off greatly when students begin to write nonfiction research pieces.

Bookmark Connections

Have students touch the stars and light bulb when they put facts and main ideas in their own words.

Name _____

 Using My Own Words

Try putting ideas from a book in your own words!

Book title: _____

Author: _____

Copy one fact from this page or book.

☆ _____

_____

_____

_____

_____

_____

Who is the author of that fact?

_____

(the book's author)

When I find a fact in a book, it belongs to that book's author. I want to remember the facts in my own words.

Now rewrite that fact using your own words.

☆ _____

_____

_____

_____

It's hard to write facts in my own words. I look away from the book and ask myself what the author is trying to say.

53

Lesson Page

Which Facts Are Most Important?

Overview:
It can be challenging for students to name the most important facts after reading a text. In this activity, students look at the heading and first sentence to help determine key ideas.

Before Using This Organizer:
Make copies of page 55 for students to complete. Choose a nonfiction book with clear headings and strong topic sentences.

Directions:
(1) Model this activity for the class. Read aloud one section of the book you have chosen. List three facts on the board or whiteboard. Make sure two of the facts relate directly to the heading or main idea of the section. Include a third fact that is interesting, but less important to the main idea.

(2) Explain that you are going to look back at the facts you listed to see which ones are most important. Share with students that one way to identify important facts is to see which facts support the heading(s) on the page. Draw attention to the heading, pointing out any ways in which it stands out from other text (boldface, colorful type, all capitals, etc.). Read aloud the topic sentence (often the sentence that follows the heading).

(3) Think aloud as you decide which facts best support the heading and topic sentence. Put an *H* next to these facts on the board.

(4) Distribute the graphic organizer and repeat the activity for a different section in the book, this time encouraging students to work more independently. Read the new section aloud and have students list three facts. Then reread the heading and topic sentence and have students put an *H* next to facts that best support them.

Nonfiction

Name James Gavin

Which Facts Are Most Important?

Book title: What Is a Plant?

Author: Bobbie Kalman

List three facts from the section you just read.

☆ Most living things on Earth depend on plants. H

☆ Plants give people and animals food. H

☆ Plants clean the air by making oxygen. H

The most important facts are the ones that match the topic of the section. The heading tells you the topic. Write the heading of this section:
Living things need plants

Now reread the facts that you listed.

Put an **H** in front of facts that connect to the heading.

55

Bookmark Connections

Have students touch the stars when they name facts. Have them touch the slice of watermelon when naming the heading.

Name _____

Which Facts Are Most Important?

Book title: _____

Author: _____

List three facts from the section you just read.

 _____

_____

_____

_____

_____

_____

The most important facts are the ones that match the topic of the section
The heading tells you the topic. Write the heading of this section:

_____

Now reread the facts that you listed.

Put an **H** in front of facts that connect to the heading.

Lesson Page

Now I Wonder...

Overview:
Asking questions is an important—and natural—part of being an active reader. In this activity, students will generate questions as they read a nonfiction text.

Before Using This Organizer:
Make copies of page 57 for students to complete. Choose a nonfiction book on a topic about which students are not likely to have a lot of prior knowledge.

Directions:
① Ask students if they have ever thought of questions during or after reading. Point out that asking questions is a strategy many readers use to keep track of what they are learning. Some questions are answered later on in the same book. If a question is not answered in the book, readers can check other places to satisfy their curiosity.

② Share an example of questioning. For example, ask students to imagine that they are reading a book about snails and encounter the fact that snails' shells grow with them. Point out that this makes you wonder what snails' shells are made of. Ask students what questions come to mind for them.

③ Distribute the graphic organizer and introduce the book that you have selected for today. Explain that as you read, you want students to jot down two new facts that they learn and two questions that occur to them.

Read the book or section aloud, pausing after each paragraph to ask students if the facts ___de them ask any questions.

___ students' completed organizers after reading. Ask students if any ___ ___stions were answered as you kept reading. If so, have them put ___ next to that question.

___nts to record questions any time they are reading. ___f their reading-response or writing notebook

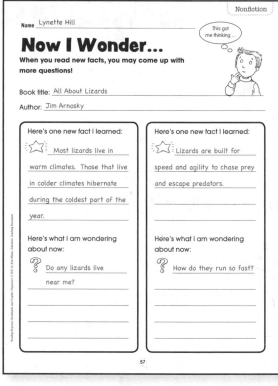

Bookmark Connections

Have students touch the whole watermelon when naming the title, the stars when sharing facts, and the question mark when stating their questions.

Name _____

This got me thinking ...

Now I Wonder...

When you read new facts, you may come up with more questions!

Book title: _____

Author: _____

Here's one new fact I learned:

☆ _____

_____

_____

_____

_____

Here's what I am wondering about now:

❓ _____

_____

_____

_____

Here's one new fact I learned:

☆ _____

_____

_____

_____

_____

Here's what I am wondering about now:

❓ _____

_____

_____

_____

Lesson Page
Find the Main Idea

Overview:
While students are sometimes in a rush to read on, stopping to identify the main idea in the text is an effective way to boost comprehension. In this activity, students will find the main idea and key supporting details in a text.

Before Using This Organizer:
Make copies of page 59 for students to complete. Choose a nonfiction book to share.

Directions:

① Review what students know about main idea. Explain that the main idea is the most important idea in the book or on the page. Point out that other ideas in the book or on the page often tell more about the main idea. These are called supporting details. Offer an example or two to make sure students understand:

Main Idea: Dogs help people in many ways.

Supporting detail: Some dogs act as "eyes" for the blind.

Supporting detail: Some dogs work on farms.

Supporting detail: Some dogs rescue people who are lost or hurt.

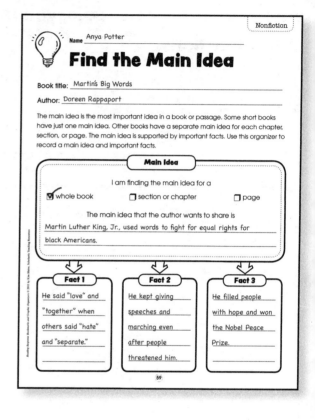

② Distribute the graphic organizer and review the directions. Explain that you want students to think about the main idea and supporting details in the text they are about to hear.

③ Tell students whether you will be reading a whole book, chapter/section, or single page. Have them record the type of text, along with the book title and author, on the organizer.

④ Read the text. Afterward, ask students if they can tell what the book, page, or section was mostly about. If necessary, call attention to the title or section heading as a clue. Once students have arrived at the main idea, have them record it on the organizer.

⑤ Challenge students to recall important supporting details from the read-aloud. Have them add three details to the organizer.

Teaching Tip:
For some students, it can be challenging to name the main idea right after reading a piece. Try having students name the three important facts first, then articulate the main idea.

Bookmark Connections

Have students touch the light bulb when naming the main idea and the three stars when naming the facts.

Name _____

Find the Main Idea

Book title: _____

Author: _____

The main idea is the most important idea in a book or passage. Some short books have just one main idea. Other books have a separate main idea for each chapter, section, or page. The main idea is supported by important facts. Use this organizer to record a main idea and important facts.

Main Idea

I am finding the main idea for a

☐ whole book ☐ section or chapter ☐ page

The main idea that the author wants to share is

_____

_____

Fact 1

_____

_____

_____

_____

Fact 2

_____

_____

_____

_____

Fact 3

_____

_____

_____

_____

Lesson Page

Author's Purpose

Overview:

Every nonfiction piece is written for a reason. Sometimes the author's purpose is obvious, but at other times, it is harder to identify. In this activity, students will learn to find the author's purpose in a text.

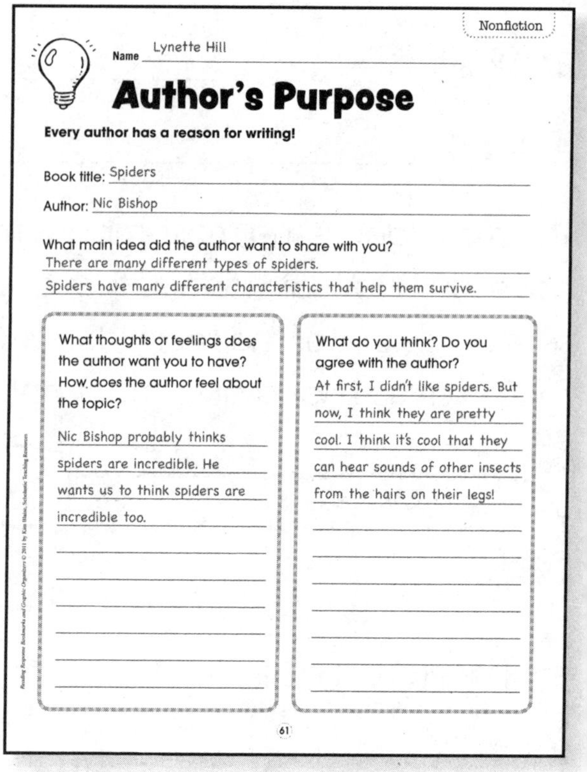

Before Using This Organizer:

Make copies of page 61 for students to complete. Choose a nonfiction book to share.

Directions:

① Review some of the reasons people write. Explain that nonfiction authors usually write to inform (share facts) or explain (tell how or why something happens). The author may also want to share with readers his or her feeling or opinion about a topic. For example, he or she might want to show that the rainforest is important to protect or that spiders are really cool.

② Explain that the class is going to work together to figure out an author's purpose for writing a nonfiction text. Show students the book you will be reading and have them record the title and author.

③ Point out that the main idea is an important clue to the author's purpose. It shows the big idea that the author wanted to get across. Challenge students to listen for the main idea as you begin reading.

④ Have students name the main idea and record it on the graphic organizer. Then, ask students if they can guess the author's opinion about the topic. Have them record this as well, if an opinion was apparent.

⑤ At the right of the organizer, have students add a sentence or two telling whether they agree with the author's opinion.

Teaching Tip:

After doing this once as a group lesson, try having students complete the organizer in pairs. Have both partners read the same text. Then have them discuss their ideas about author's purpose as they complete the page.

Worksheet (sample, right side):

Nonfiction

Name Lynette Hill

Author's Purpose

Every author has a reason for writing!

Book title: Spiders

Author: Nic Bishop

What main idea did the author want to share with you?
There are many different types of spiders.
Spiders have many different characteristics that help them survive.

What thoughts or feelings does the author want you to have? How does the author feel about the topic?	What do you think? Do you agree with the author?
Nic Bishop probably thinks spiders are incredible. He wants us to think spiders are incredible too.	At first, I didn't like spiders. But now, I think they are pretty cool. I think it's cool that they can hear sounds of other insects from the hairs on their legs!

61

Bookmark Connections

Have students touch the whole watermelon when naming the title and author and the light bulb when naming the main idea.

Name _____

Author's Purpose

Every author has a reason for writing!

Book title: _____

Author: _____

What main idea did the author want to share with you?

_____

_____

What thoughts or feelings does the author want you to have? How does the author feel about the topic?

_____

_____

_____

_____

_____

_____

_____

What do you think? Do you agree with the author?

_____

_____

_____

_____

_____

_____

_____

_____

_____

_____

Lesson Page
Text Features

Overview:
Nonfiction texts have many features—headings, boldface type, photos, captions, and so on—that can help readers deepen their understanding of a topic. In this activity, you will help students not only to identify those features but also to understand how each feature can make them better readers.

Before Using This Organizer:
Make copies of page 63 for students to complete. Choose a nonfiction book with plenty of text features (charts, photos, headings) to share. Have a supply of other nonfiction books on hand for students to use for steps 2 and 3.

Directions:
(1) Hold up the nonfiction book you have chosen and have students notice the various text features. Discuss how each one helps the reader. For example:

> A photo might show what an animal looks like.

> A chart might give additional facts in an easy-to-read format.

> Headings divide facts into sections and give hints about the main idea.

(2) Have students select a nonfiction book from your classroom library. Distribute the graphic organizer and review the directions. Have each student select one page in his or her book and check off all of the text features the page has to offer.

(3) Have students pick one text feature on the page to examine more closely. Have them sketch the feature on the graphic organizer and write a few sentences describing what the text feature adds to the page. Ask: *How does it help you as a reader?*

(4) If you wish, make a tally of which text features your students found on their book pages.

Teaching Tip:
Save old magazines throughout the year. When you study text features, have students use the magazines to cut out examples of text features and create their own collection. Remind students that they need to identify the feature and figure out why it's on the page.

Bookmark Connections

Have students touch the whole watermelon when naming the title and author. Have students touch the stars when they name the facts they learn from the text features.

Name _____

Text Features

Nonfiction books have some special features. Which ones can you find?

Book title: _____

Author: _____

Page: _____

What text features are on this page? (Check all the features you see.)

___ Heading   ___ Photograph   ___ Graph

___ Bold or colorful text   ___ Caption   ___ Diagram

___ Map   ___ Chart   ___ Illustration

Choose one text feature to examine. What feature did you pick?

_____

Draw a picture of the text feature.

What does this feature teach you? Why is it on this page?

_____

_____

Notes